MISTER MARTINI

Mister Martini

poems by
Richard Carr

2007 Winner, Vassar Miller Prize in Poetry

University of North Texas Press
Denton, Texas

10 9 8 7 6 5 4 3 2 1

Permissions:
University of North Texas Press
P.O. Box 311336
Denton, TX 76203-1336

The paper used in this book meets the minimum requirements
of the American National Standard for Permanence of Paper for
Printed Library Materials, z39.48.1984. Binding materials have
been chosen for durability.

Library of Congress Cataloging-in-Publication Data

Carr, Richard, 1962–
Mister Martini : poems / by Richard Carr.
p. cm. — (Vassar Miller Prize in poetry series ; 15)
"2007 Winner, Vassar Miller Prize in Poetry."
ISBN 978-1-57441-242-0 (pbk. : alk. paper)
1. Fathers and sons--Poetry. I. Title.
PS3603.A77433M57 2008
811'.6—dc22
2007039943

Mister Martini is Number 15 in the Vassar Miller Prize in Poetry Series.

CONTENTS

INVENTOR

My father was an inventor of martinis.
He acquired archaic languages,
collected Renaissance textiles.
But mostly he made martinis.

He worked at night in a closed room.

§

Martini chilled among purple crocuses,
served with two drops of spring snow
gathered from the petals.

SHADOW

In my room I watched the tree shadow
on the window during lightning storms,
thinking the twigs looked like
skeleton fingers

pointing at something,
urgent.

§

Martini with a boy and a girl in it
swimming nude, their nipples hard
in the cold, aromatic mist.

MATHEMATICS

I took an interest in mathematics,
the vacant lot
where DNA plants its garden
and the slow bees bathe

in sun-glossed forgetfulness.

§

Martini of cyclonic color,
yellow and green songbirds
rocketing

upward through fire-black pines.

Ivy

In the house bearded with ivy,
there was a man with him.
I turned on the television and listened,
slouching in the slack-jaw yoga of boyhood

as the pushing and shoving of their tussle
shook the wall.

§

Martini with a granule of sugar
submerged in the taut liquid,
an alien sentience

suspended
in the conic space of its vessel.

FREIGHTCAR

Clinging to the windy undercarriage of freightcar sleep,
I woke
abruptly in those days—sometimes
miles from home.

§

Martini nostalgic
for the small sandwiches and sweetened
milk of its youth.

HANDS

I went to him with cupped hands.
While he ate, the crumbs in his lap
rolled in the folds of his black slacks
like feudal warriors rushing into battle

and retreating down rain-soaked hills.
When the dessert trolley rolled into view,
I closed my hands and lowered my head.

§

Martini descending by elevator
into the earth
with a caged, silent canary

who knows his role
is to blacken and die.

PLAZA

The figure skaters at the plaza rink
dazzled us with their anguish,
black banners of revolt,
and shattered ice,

while my father urinated on himself.
I tried to continue his work then.

§

Martini with silver hair still thick
and blue eyes rubbed to translucence
turning to its son and saying:

You are a martini circling the park
in the back of a cab, slouching,
always risking the spill, you

with your dark glasses and crisp olive.

ATOMS

We were like atoms smashed together
creating dazzling light and destruction.

§

Martini made of tears
squeezed from the eyes of pimps.

PLAY

I began to think of my father as childlike.
His late-night ruminations
a play of footsteps acted out upstairs,
I did not know his greatness.

I pulled my hands into my sleeves.

§

Martini dogsledding across Alaska,
wind-tears crystallizing
as they fling loose in the blinding sun.

ANT

In my recurring dream I was an ant
baking on the pavement,
my movements erratic,
commanded by an erratic will

hiding in a tiny cave complex
beneath the peonies—
sweet peonies!—
and our murdering enemy approaching

in heavy black shoes.

§

Martini throwing open the window
with a sudden wash of air
many times through the morning obsessively

drawing breath into the house.

SUMMER

On a summer day in the park,
when he was not old and I was not young,
we leaned over the rail of the footbridge
and looked into the green lagoon,

our faces rippling together.

§

Martini made from the nectar
of a hundred pink peonies
gathered by a thousand black ants

working silently in the dense perfume.

CUISINE

He toasted the local cuisine
even as his digestive tract deteriorated.
Blood and feces leaked from him,
but he refused

to look down.
Gold coins poured into his raised cup,
and men saluted him—
so brilliant was his gaze.

§

Martini tattooed
with a smiling sun-disc,
yellow-haired, benevolent,

white-hot on the tongue.

DIRT

At times I thought he would recover.
I couldn't help him, of course,
couldn't compete.
I kissed his cheek and tasted dirt.

§

Martini holding a gun to its head,
looking out a heavily draped window,
the first snowflakes of November swirling

through the dark arms of the naked elms.

ODOMETER

In the last limping mile of his beat-up life
the old man's odometer simply
rolled over
and he drove on into yet another reality,

now hissing and steaming,
now fast and new.

§

Martini admiring a bowl of sliced
strawberries
gathering all the red, wet

light in the room
to itself.

TELEVISION

I watched the midday news on television
standing up
in case I should need to take action.
Or turn away.

Sometimes I saw my father on television—
once on the jumbo screen downtown
with stock prices scrolling across his chest
like war medals.

§

Martini wearing a black suit sleekly,
white shirt pried open, the exposed flesh
exuding cigarette smoke and woody cologne,

turning to its son and saying:
You are a martini chilled in the street,
arms crossed, hands clamped in the hollows,

head bobbing downward against the wind,
the eyes two lolling pearl onions
gone pungent.

WIND

I was like a quiet day,
polite
and sunny at the dinner table,
sometimes

bursting into the conversation
like a gust of gritty wind in the eyes.

§

Martini with a scudding cloud
over a painted sea—
light struggling with dark,

a lilac and lavender sea.

FALCON

I wanted to reconcile with my father.
I told him I was a falcon
like him.
In answer

his eyes rose to the sky
and did not come down.

§

Martini of dark pond-water
with an emerald damselfly on the rim
exercising its wings languidly.

CAR

Every year he drove a new car
into a tree.
He was an actuarial constant,
and I loved him all the more

for his dreary predictability.

§

Martini made of golden pollen,
visited by a fat, fuzzy, drunken bee
deeply calm

as he merges
with his mirror image on the surface.

SEQUENCE

I marveled at the Fibonacci sequence of his life,
the outward spiraling of his self-image,
each lie the sum of the previous two,
the self-aggrandizing accretion

a ram's horn of diabolical power.

§

Martini contemplating
the brevity of its existence,
how few words were exchanged,

the dollar dropped into the tip goblet.

CEREMONY

I followed him into the streets of his youth
to the raucous corner of 7th and 57th,
where, in a sly ceremony,
he opened a violin case on the sidewalk

and removed a bottle of gin,
a bottle of vermouth, still sealed,
a jar of green olives, pitted but not stuffed,
and a small tin of square toothpicks.

He performed
without the aid of ice, shaker or glassware,
filling his mouth directly
as he gargled a song

and made broad flourishes with his arms.

§

Martini containing a rain shower
soaking the white shirt
of a man pressing his hands to his face.

FORMULA

He was nervous about dying
and so conducted a series of laboratory trials
in search of a formula
for a memorable yet refined passing—

a death martini.

§

Martini with a time-elapsed film
of an orchid growing in the crook of a tree,
days and weeks passing in fluttering seconds,

the arc of stem
and scrolled petals curving outward
into pink, pale maturity,

then reversing,
withdrawing rapidly back into the moss,
leaving only the scent,

a powdery, salty aftertaste
of dried milk.

THISTLE

As a young man he was a thistle,
purple-topped, strong in the cold night
as he strode home from the dance clubs in shirtsleeves
and hard shoes

and sullen, spitting anger.

§

Martini made of mercury,
flecks of coal,
a nail.

SNAIL

His soul lived in a snail shell
hidden in his vest pocket.
We did not talk about it—
so small, really, it was nothing.

I knew of people who ate souls
as a delicacy.
I had heard the little, stolen soul-voices
crying in the cannibals' heads,

and yet I did not question the bad breath
of my father's formalized kisses,
left cheek, right,
though the lingering, buttery odor

was hot in my face.

§

Martini composed of the humid night
in a trash-strewn neighborhood,
spots of blood on the pavement,

an engine idling.

GODS

I worshipped the gods of our city
in my father's place,
bearing to their altars
offerings of crusty bread and marbled cheese.

Although he believed in the deities—
the God of Mercy and Humiliation,
the Oracle of Horsemanship and Enterprise,
the Golden Idol of Cancer, Tongues, and Weeping—

he despised them all as competitors and louts.

§

Martini observing the city from a great height
as the lights come on in the apartment towers
and darkness fills the lamp-dotted park,

squinting at the old marquees
that glitter and wink in the long street-canyons,
whorish,

turning to its son and saying:
You are a martini admired only
by the ruined and the thirsty,

a clear, pure libation,
garnished insipidly
with a chrome-plated bullet.

EXPLOSION

I mixed my own martinis,
grinding powders, distilling essences,
often frustrated,
smashing test tubes and stemware,

my peppered hair an explosion.

§

Martini transmuting
grain alcohol
into gin of polished argent,

vermouth into shimmering
aether,
a green olive into jade sweetness.

CARDS

Destroying a deck of playing cards
carefully
I cut out all the letters and numbers
and sewed the little red and black chits together

in two long charm chains
wound around each other in a double helix
shellacked
and stood precariously on end.

For this my school gave me the science prize,
then took it away.

§

Martini designed by Vivaldi
who runs his finger around the rim
to hear it play.

HOSPITAL

Every time he went into the hospital
I wanted to pull the plug,
let his eyes stare up at the ceiling forever,
his mouth hang open in a question.

§

Martini with amber-bodied ants
crawling on a powdery white tablecloth
among crystal stems.

MURDER-SUICIDE

It was murder-suicide:
We both wanted him dead.
But neither of us could do it.
We clung to the material world—

our hats, our shoes—
doubting there was anything else.
We clung to each other.

§

Martini asking for death
from a doctor
whose amused smile

remains in place.

BOUTIQUE

He examined his reflection in boutique windows
as he strode past them in top-hat pomposity.
I stood in the tailor's doorway in my chalked suit
studying this behavior,

my legs twitching in jerky rhythm
with his stupendous strides.

§

Martini of betrayal
made of kerosene
and a cigarette butt.

CREDITORS

He socialized with my creditors,
spoke my name too casually—
with arched brows—
after dinner, during cards.

§

Martini with cannonballs of molten lava
plummeting through sea water
in boiling, fiery trajectories.

Eye

He did not impede my other relationships
but watched with a yellow eye
so that I performed as much for him
as for the other in the darkened room.

§

Martini of hemp smoke
and patchouli
served in candlelight.

Toy

He made me my first toy martini.
It looked like the Statue of Liberty
hunched inside a snow-globe.
It was to stand as a model

for my boyish amateur efforts.
I later understood the gesture
as a mix
of open mockery and secret hope.

§

Martini flung from the Eiffel Tower
on a bright, windy, buoyant night.

SALAD

He considered himself morally flawless—
a salad for lunch, an hour at the gym—
but had imperiled his soul for this quality.

§

Martini with Mark Spitz
smashing across the surface,
doing the butterfly

faster than anyone in the world.

ORGAN

He wanted his eyes cryogenically preserved
in separate tanks,
his friends among the organ farmers
untrustworthy and powerful.

§

Martini displayed in a bell jar,
the hollow-pupiled olive
whitening with age.

LANGUAGE

Sometimes when he spoke to me
I did not know the language.
His tongue moved incomprehensibly
in his head, his eyes searching.

I could see the honest, fatherly concern
in the thrust and skew of his jaw.
I felt the weight of his hand on my shoulder.
I made an obedient reply

like a dog that sits.

§

Martini with a formation of tundra swans
flying a mile above it in blue space,
only the ghosts of their voices reaching the surface

and sunlight
passing through their white bodies.

ELMS

We held hands under elms in the sun.
All the leaves were yellow
and none of them had fallen.
That was the autumn I remembered.

That was the boyhood I cherished.

§

Martini breathing
cautiously
the aromas of cold rain,

trodden leaves—
brown sugar
of bottomless decay.

LIGHTNING

He stood next to a man struck by lightning
at the end of a pier where they had met
during a sleety winter storm.
The blast hit just as one of them

turned away to light a cigarette
in the calm of his cupped hands
and the other lifted his face into the rain
to wait for their talk to resume.

§

Martini no longer in love
but maintaining a cool charade.

39

ROLLER SKATES

Nothing sprouted
where I buried my roller skates.
I imagined them preserved
for millennia

though under the pressures of darkness
beaten
into a deranged form.

§

Martini polluted
by thin swirls of plant oils,
pulp,

travel in an arid railway carriage
and dealings in black-market antiquities
turning to its son and saying:

You are a martini hand-carved
of prized blue and gold-flecked lapis—
totemic, solemn—

a worthless reproduction.

Rage

My rage burned houses.
I plotted the destruction
of his precious skyscrapers.
I dreamed of his lovers

thronging in long stairwells
in the emergencies I made
against his careless scrutiny.

§

Martini reciting pi
through a hundred rapid-fire digits
to a choked halt.

Dogs

He lifted dogs by the ears.
He beamed when they smelled of soap,
encouraged loud barking.

§

Martini of urine.

SHOES

His shoes were sprawling palaces
for his imperial feet.
The chandeliers jangled as he walked.
Where he stood,

rose gardens grew
and the trees leaned toward him
in weary, weeping poses.

§

Martini buttoning its coat,
eyelids lowered
to accept an obedient kiss.

PIANO

My father worried about his piano
escaping the apartment
and wandering into the park to graze
and play low chords in the meadow.

I worried about my kitchen chairs
running away,
crossing the street alone,
incapable of holding hands.

§

Martini wearing white lipstick,
pools of mauve blood thickening
beneath the flaked skin.

SHOULDERS

I was soft,
my shoulders
avocadoes.

§

Martini shattered
between two bricks.

LOUNGE

In the darkest velvet lounge of my heart
I knew I would become him,
reject him, kill him,
and so exceed him. But not in that order.

§

Martini sipped by Socrates
surrounded by his friends.

SUBWAY

Deep in the subway system
we rode standing in an empty car.
Sometimes I held his briefcase
loaded with silverware.

§

Martini washing its armpit
with a bar of yellow soap.

Stardom

He foresaw his own dim stardom,
his diminishing.
He would grow shorter, wear smaller shoes,
flutter

his purple eyelids ever more slowly.

§

Martini moonlighting
serenely
in men's fragrances at Macy's.

UNDERWORLD

He intended to walk unescorted
into the underworld.
He would know his way
in the total darkness,

his elegant Italian loafers
crunching steadily on the cinder path.

§

Martini fed blood
through dangling tubes.

BED

I sat next to him on his bed.
He had grown so thin
at the surface
I could read a book to him

by the light of his mind.

§

Martini of needles and milk.

PERFUME

Like my morning dab of perfume,
I began to forget him
before he was actually gone.
I became concerned with my teeth.

I thought of changing my hairstyle.
I went shopping for shoes.

§

Martini with an ice-shattering headache,
hubcaps and coffee cans
thrown against barred windows in the alley,

turning to its son and saying:
You are a martini turning away,
shoulders squared,

long, black overcoat hanging
in perfect vertical folds, you
with a bright peach in your hand

and no law.

FINGERS

His fingers were long and slim,
alien-slender,
like a spider's jointed, wispy legs,
inhumanly strong at the tips.

§

Martini lifted up without effort
from the stainless bartop
into white neon.

SUPERNOVA

There were black holes of all-consuming desperation
and flashing eons of supernova genius.
I took measurements, made calculations,
but could not determine if the universe was expanding

or collapsing
or sealed in a bottle adrift on a greater sea.

§

Martini weighing the uses of a tart cherry,
a razor blade,
chocolate syrup.

SILK

He walked in the city of white silk
and green plaid,
washed his hands
in its canals

as though praying there on his knees.

§

Martini no longer moved by music
having a quiet lunch alone
to work out the future.

LIQUID

No complexity without evaporation,
he slept in a trance-state
of liquid calm
in the smallest and farthest of many rooms.

§

Martini trekking in the desert,
mumbling a melted language
of mud bricks and long-legged birds.

ORPHAN

He perpetuated the myth
of his orphan beginnings:
surviving on stale bagels,
hawking broken watches.

Chasing a blowing newspaper,
he declared himself a phoenix
that would rise again one day
from the detritus of the street.

§

Martini left out on the fire escape
to soak up moonlight.

LOBBY

When I turned my back on him
in the hospital lobby
he threw a mock tantrum
and laughed.

He pretended to strangle himself.

§

Martini of springtime,
gray gutter slush,
tar speckled.

BREATHING

Forty-two city blocks distant,
he listened to my breathing as I lay
alert in my bed.
I imagined him standing

naked in the darkness of his room,
a pale receptor.

§

Martini sealed in a coffin
under heavy earth,
air thickening with its odor,

alcohol, juniper, evergreen solvent.

FOG

At a party honoring his longevity
his head turned into a fog machine.
The mists rolled down over his shoulders
like the long white hairs of the dead.

He toasted his own achievements.
His hand shook,
and he spilled on his wrist.
And yet he stood placidly

above the eerie weather he had made.

§

Martini flying above the clouds
in the pressurized cabin
of its ingratitude.

STREET

He was a jubilant walker.
He walked every street,
and the street swirled in his wake:
voices, chiming laughter, friends meeting.

Then the traffic closed in behind him
and the cab horns honked their bad music.

§

Martini watching from a doorway,
swirling with love and pride
and dizzy, empty grief.

STREAM

Sometimes I fell all the way back to the beginning,
boyhood a stream
running fast deep clear tumbling alive.

§

Martini poured into the river
from a high bridge
vibrating with heavy traffic.

ELEVATOR

In a rising elevator
his eyes went white.
Few in his retinue
noticed the rising

pitch in his voice.

§

Martini made of skyline,
helicopter,
and a single phobia

impaled on a toothpick.

HUSK

I wore the husk of Mister Martini.
An old snakeskin suit,
it crackled
as I walked stiff-legged.

§

Martini of spidery dryness,
dust, pollen, spores
on puffs of wind.

CLAMS

Over a dinner of clams,
only clams,
I bragged to him that I would succeed
where he had failed,

and he replied dryly: Then you will do nothing.
But it hurt him
to know I had made an account of his failures.
He tapped a shell with his cocktail fork.

It angered him.

§

Martini with something to prove
on the tennis court—bony legs, flabby arm,
bulging eye.

POKER

He played poker with the all-knowing gods.
Laughed in their faces.
Slapped his cards on the table.
Lost his shirt.

§

Martini thirsting for one
more cool sip of life.

Breeze

I lay in his bed
and spread him over me
like a cotton sheet billowed
on a hot night

for the breeze it would bring.